HOW RUDE!

10 REAL BUGS WHO WON'T MIND THEIR MANNERS

by
Heather L. Montgomery
Illustrated by
Howard McWilliam

Scholastic Inc.

FOR DR. JOELLA KILLIAN, WHO OPENED MY EYES TO THE JOYS OF BUG-WATCHING.

With special thanks to the scientists who made this book possible:
Judith Becerra, Omar Tonsi Eldakar, Brian Forschler, Roy Gratz,
Sanford Porter, Brett Ratcliffe, Inon Scharf, Per Terje Smiseth,
José Roberto Trigo, David Wagner, and Martha R. Weiss.

Photos ©: back cover: Michael Dykstra/Dreamstime; 7: Margarethe Brummermann;
8: Jack Clark/AgStock/Design Pics; 11: Doug Wechsler; 12: Bill Beatty/Visuals Unlimited;
15: Henrik Larsson/Thinkstock; 16: Courtesy Rudolf H. Scheffrahn/University of Florida;
19 top, 19 center: Minden Pictures/Masterfile; 20: Nature's Images/Science Source;
23: S.D. Porter, USDA-ARS; 24: Courtesy James Lindsey; 26: S.D. Porter, USDA-ARS.

ISBN 978-0-545-78055-1

Copyright © 2015 by Scholastic Inc.

12 11 10 9 8 7 6 5 4 3 2 1   15 16 17 18 19 20

Printed in the U.S.A.   40

First printing, September 2015

Art Direction by Paul W. Banks
Design by Kay Petronio

Some bugs litter. Some pass gas. Others throw poop.

In this book, you will find ten of the rudest, crudest KID bugs around.

Why are they uncivil?

Why won't they mind their manners?

Will they ever GROW UP?

SEE IF YOU CAN FIGURE IT OUT.

Kid bugs

Young bugs are everywhere, have all the headaches of being a kid — just a little more extreme. Instead of growing out of clothes, they grow out of their skin. If they don't act right, they face more than a mad momma. Skip cleaning their room? They could get the death penalty.

Besides, their bodies keep on changing. As they grow up, some insects go through the four stages of complete metamorphosis: egg, larva, pupa, adult. Butterflies and beetles do that. Other bugs go through the three stages of incomplete metamorphosis: egg, nymph, adult. Scale insects and giant mesquite bugs do that.

The "Battle for the Grossest"

AZALEA
CATERPILLAR

EASTERN
SUBTERRANEAN
TERMITE

Meet the kid
contestants . . .

SILVER-
SPOTTED
SKIPPER
CATERPILLAR

DECAPITATING
FLY

SAN
JOSE SCALE

AMERICAN BURYING BEETLE

GIANT MESQUITE BUG

SOUTHERN GOLDEN TORTOISE BEETLE

ANTLION

WATER STRIDER

THE RESULTS ARE IN . . . .

5

GROSS-O-METER

NAUSEATING · REPULSIVE · ATROCIOUS · SHOCKING · FOUL · NASTY

MANNERS METER

Gassy Guy #10
(GIANT MESQUITE BUG, *THASUS NEOCALIFORNICUS*)

A YOUNG MESQUITE BUG seems like a popular guy, just hanging out with his buds . . . until he lets one rip. Phew! Now the air stinks of skunk and burned plastic. Everyone splits, as if he's just farted.

BAKED BEANS

What's the Stink?

Actually, the mesquite bug didn't fart at all. This young bug, called a nymph, released gas from glands along the sides of his body, not from his tail end. Like a fart, though, the compounds in the gas spread through the air and reek.

By making a stink, the nymph probably saved everyone's lives. A praying mantis had just stalked up, ready to snag tasty mesquite bugs for supper. The nymph's gas was a silent message to his friends: "Scatter!" When the mesquite bugs spread out, it is harder for the praying mantis to catch any of them. The raunchy gas can even kill a mantis. Strong stuff!

THE REAL DEAL:

GROSS-O-METER

NAUSEATING
REPULSIVE
ATROCIOUS
SHOCKING
RUDE
NASTY

MANNERS METER

Pest Guest

#9

(SAN JOSE SCALE, *QUADRASPIDIOTUS PERNICIOSUS*)

THE SAN JOSE SCALE

insect is such a rude guest — and a total couch potato — you'd never want to invite this kid over. If he did come to visit, he'd just plop down and refuse to budge — or do *anything*! All day, he'd slurp sugary sap from your tree and overstay his welcome.

He's so lazy. How lazy? So lazy he doesn't even notice when he loses his antennae and legs!

THE REAL DEAL:

Lost Limbs

It takes energy to keep six legs and two antennae working properly. As the San Jose scale nymph grows, he molts, shedding his skin and changing his body shape. When he does this, he does not regrow his unused body parts. This saves him energy.

Don't worry, when he becomes an adult, he'll regrow his body parts. Male scale insects need them to move around and find the females. The females, however, never get their legs back!

GROSS-O-METER

NAUSEATING
NASTY
REPULSIVE
RUDE
ATROCIOUS
SHOCKING
MANNERS METER

Quiet Riot #8 (AZALEA CATERPILLAR, DATANA MAJOR)

AZALEA CATERPILLARS

may look peaceful, but touch one and you may start a riot. He'll rear his head up, raise his rump, and jerk his whole body. That'll set off his buddies. Pretty soon you have a mob of bugs break dancing.

If poky legs, spiky hair, and a throbbing mass don't scare you, he's got more. He'll ooze spit from one end of his body and green goo from the other.

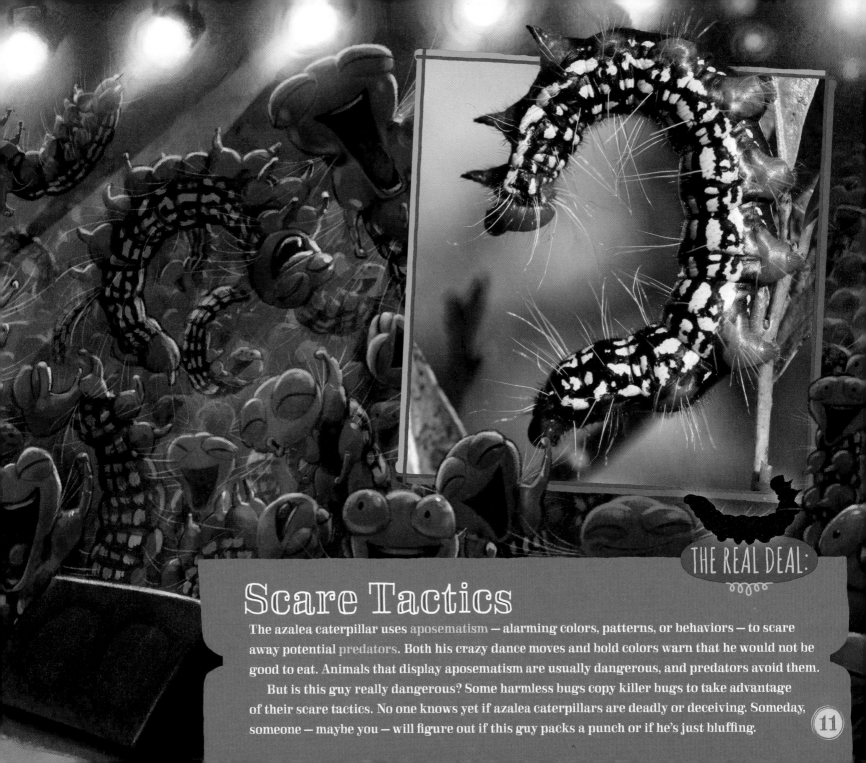

Scare Tactics

The azalea caterpillar uses aposematism — alarming colors, patterns, or behaviors — to scare away potential predators. Both his crazy dance moves and bold colors warn that he would not be good to eat. Animals that display aposematism are usually dangerous, and predators avoid them.

But is this guy really dangerous? Some harmless bugs copy killer bugs to take advantage of their scare tactics. No one knows yet if azalea caterpillars are deadly or deceiving. Someday, someone — maybe you — will figure out if this guy packs a punch or if he's just bluffing.

11

GROSS-O-METER

NASTY · NAUSEATING · REPULSIVE · ATROCIOUS · SHOCKING · RUDE

MANNERS METER

Litter Bug

#7

(ANTLION, *MYRMELEON IMMACULATUS*)

THE ANTLION

has no respect for Mother Nature. For dinner, this kid traps ants in a funnel-shaped pit. When he finishes his meal of ant guts, he tosses the trash out the front door. The litter junks up his yard, but he doesn't even care.

What's the Scoop?

Like all bugs, ants wear their skeletons on the outside of their bodies. Their exoskeleton is too tough for many predators to chomp through. The antlion larva has a sneaky way around this little problem. First, he stabs his pointy jaws through the exoskeleton. Then, he squirts in a juice that turns the ant's insides to mush. Finally, he sucks it all out.

Since the larva has no way to chew up the exoskeleton, and no place to store it, he has to toss it. Fortunately, nature slowly recycles it through the process of decomposition.

13

GROSS-O-METER

NAUSEATING
REPULSIVE
ATROCIOUS
SHOCKING
RUDE
NASTY

MANNERS METER

Poop Suit

#6

(SOUTHERN GOLDEN TORTOISE BEETLE, *CHARIDOTELLA SEXPUNCTATA BICOLOR*)

THE TORTOISE BEETLE LARVA wears poop! When most bugs have to "go," they drop their dung in the dirt and let it turn back into soil. Not this guy! He refuses to let his poop go. Instead, he stockpiles it on his back.

SCHOOL BUS

Protective Poo?

The larva of a tortoise beetle has a flexible hook at the end of his abdomen. He uses it to add his pasty poo to the crusty covering on his back. When he sheds his skin, he adds that to his back, too.

Scientists guessed that these beetle larvae were using their poop like shields for protection. They decided to test their hypothesis. The scientists pulled the poop off some larvae but left it on others. Then they dropped the larvae in with predators like carpenter ants and chickens. An equal number of poop-covered and clean larvae were eaten. So, they still didn't know for sure why these guys wear their poo.

Doo-Doo Diner #5

(EASTERN SUBTERRANEAN TERMITE, *RETICULITERMES FLAVIPES*)

GROSS-O-METER
NAUSEATING
REPULSIVE
ATROCIOUS
SHOCKING
RUDE
NASTY
MANNERS METER

TERMITE NYMPHS

go all out for the gross stuff. They like ABC food — that's Already Been Chewed! They take it right from their friend's mouth.

But there's more. . . . To get the best stuff, a termite nymph puts his mouth up to his buddy's behind and gulps down a sticky mush. Delish!

Belly Buddies

Termites eat wood, but without some help, their bodies cannot handle the tough wood. To break down the wood, termites depend on microbes, microscopic organisms that live inside the termites' guts. The termites supply the food and the microbes turn it into energy — a win-win situation.

But when a termite nymph molts, he sheds his skin plus the lining of his gut. That means he loses his microbes, too. If he ate wood immediately after that, it would sit in his belly and give him a tummy ache.

So, a freshly molted nymph grabs breakfast from the rear end of a friend. The milky material is full of microbes that settle down in his guts and get to work. What he eats is not *really* doo-doo, but it comes from the same place!

GROSS-O-METER

NASTY
NAUSEATING
REPULSIVE
RUDE
ATROCIOUS
SHOCKING

MANNERS METER

Upchuck Eater (AMERICAN BURYING BEETLE, *NICROPHORUS AMERICANUS*)

#4

THE BURYING BEETLES LARVAE live next door to their meal — a dead bird soaked in spit. But still, these lazy guys nag their parents. They demand room service! Whenever Mom or Pop Beetle comes by, the kids beat on their parents' shells. Tap, tap, tap. The parents are pushovers and barf up some dead meat.

Dead Body Delight

Instead of wasting time hunting live animals, burying beetle parents take advantage of fast food — dead animals, called carrion. They just pull up to a dead body, bury it, and lay eggs in the soil nearby. They carve a bowl into the top of the carrion and fill it with saliva to soften the tough meat. Then, the eggs hatch and the young beg for food. The parents eat some meat and spit it back up to feed the larvae.

Sadly, the American burying beetle is endangered. One reason their numbers have dropped: not enough dead bodies to go around. Lots of animals compete for carrion.

GROSS-O-METER

NAUSEATING
REPULSIVE
ATROCIOUS
SHOCKING
RUDE
NASTY

MANNERS METER

Feces Flicker #3

(SILVER-SPOTTED SKIPPER CATERPILLAR, *EPARGYREUS CLARUS*)

THE SKIPPER CATERPILLAR, who lives in a cute house made of a leaf, seems like such a civil guy. But at potty time, his nasty nature comes out. He sticks his rear out the back door and shoots his poop wherever he pleases.

He can flick his feces up to 62 inches (158 cm). That's like you flinging your poop from the 50-yard line into the end zone!

Stinky Stuff

Why do they flick? The skippers aren't cleaning their rooms to keep their mothers happy. They do it because the stuff stinks.

When the caterpillars are tucked away in poop-free rooms, predatory wasps fly right by them without taking notice. But when a wasp smells caterpillar poo, she heads straight for it. The wasp is not coming over for a chat — she's ready to chow down on some caterpillar. The food chain in action!

GROSS-O-METER / MANNERS METER

NASTY · NAUSEATING · REPULSIVE · ATROCIOUS · SHOCKING · RUDE

Lurker & Slurper

(DECAPITATING FLY, *PSEUDACTEON LITORALIS*)

#2

A FLY LARVA lurks inside a fire ant's head. When the time is right, he enjoys a good meal — a sloppy serving of ant brains. Slurp! No one hassles him about his table manners so he goes one step further. He makes the ant's head fall off! Then he squirms around inside that giant bowl of a head, sucking up every last drop.

Hungry Hero

A mother decapitating fly stabs a fire ant and shoots in an egg like a torpedo. Inside the ant's body, the egg hatches and the hungry larva lives on ant blood. When he is old enough, the larva moves into the ant's head and releases a chemical that loosens it. Plop. The head drops to the ground. After an easy meal of everything left inside, the fly larva uses the empty ant head as a safe place to hide as he grows into an adult.

Decapitating flies might be gross, but scientists are turning them into heroes. Fire ants are spreading across North America where they don't belong. Those ants have a nasty sting that can cause a severe reaction in people who are allergic. Decapitating flies only attack fire ants. So scientists are releasing these flies to kill off the fire ants.

GROSS-O-METER
MANNERS METER
NAUSEATING
REPULSIVE
ATROCIOUS
SHOCKING
RUDE
NASTY

The Cannibal

(WATER STRIDER, *GERRIS PINGREENSIS*)

#1

A WATER STRIDER skates across the surface of the pond. This guy's hungry. He feels the water for little ripples that might indicate a juicy bug fell in . . . but nothing's wiggling.

Hours later: still no other kinds of bugs in sight. He's starving! The only things moving are other water striders.

No problem!

He slides over to another strider. He grabs her. He stabs her.

THE REAL DEAL:
Strider Sandwich

Water strider nymphs usually eat other kinds of bugs. However, when the food supply is low or if a large strider comes across a smaller one, striders may eat each other. A feeding strider uses tiny claws to hold its prey while poking its needlelike mouth deep inside.

Believe it or not, cannibalism can help an insect population. When a population is overcrowded, there is not enough food to go around. After some bugs are eaten, there are fewer mouths to feed. The bugs who survive have a greater chance of getting enough to eat.

Adapt or Die

So, why do all of these kid bugs act so rude? It's all about survival. A bug's got to do what a bug's got to do. Whether sucking the guts out of another bug, living inside another bug's head, or eating vomit, each behavior is an adaptation for survival.

LARVA

EGG

THE REAL DEAL:

"Bad" Behavior?

Insect behavior isn't "bad" or even "rude." Those are values that people have assigned to certain behaviors. Humans created manners so that we can get along with one another. Insects don't need to be polite, but they do need to survive. Those who survive pass their traits on to the next generation — a generation of kid bugs who will be just as gross as their parents!

PUPA

ADULT

See for Yourself!

If you think these kids are cool, go outside and find the real deal! The bugs in this book (or their close relatives) can be found in many parts of North America. To figure out if a bug is young or old, look for wings. Bugs don't get their wings till they grow up.

NICKNAME: Water strider
SCIENTIFIC NAME: Gerris pingreensis
LIFE STAGE: Nymph
HOMETOWN*: Edmonton, Canada
LENGTH: 8 mm
FAVORITE FOOD: Injured dragonflies
THREATS TO SURVIVAL: Other water striders

NICKNAME: American burying beetle
SCIENTIFIC NAME: Nicrophorus americanus
LIFE STAGE: Larva
HOMETOWN*: North Platte, NE
LENGTH: 20 mm
FAVORITE FOOD: Pheasant
THREATS TO SURVIVAL: Habitat disturbance, competition with flies

NICKNAME: San Jose scale
SCIENTIFIC NAME: Quadraspidiotus perniciosus
LIFE STAGE: Larva
HOMETOWN*: San Jose, CA
LENGTH: 0.24 mm
FAVORITE FOOD: Apples, pears
THREATS TO SURVIVAL: Parasitic wasp, cold

NICKNAME: Giant mesquite bug
SCIENTIFIC NAME: Thasus neocalifornicus
LIFE STAGE: Nymph (5TH INSTAR)
HOMETOWN*: Tucson, AZ
LENGTH: 25 mm
FAVORITE FOOD: Mesquite tree seed pods
THREATS TO SURVIVAL: Lizards, birds

NICKNAME: Decapitating fly
SCIENTIFIC NAME: Pseudacteon litoralis
LIFE STAGE: Larva
HOMETOWN*: Texas
LENGTH: 1.2 mm
FAVORITE FOOD: Fire ant
THREATS TO SURVIVAL: Fire ants

*These hometowns represent one place within a larger range where each bug can be found.

NICKNAME: Southern golden tortoise beetle
SCIENTIFIC NAME: *Charidotella sexpunctata bicolor*
LIFE STAGE: Larva
HOMETOWN*: Columbus, OH
LENGTH: 10 MM
FAVORITE FOOD: Sweet potato and morning glory leaves
THREATS TO SURVIVAL: Ladybugs, Damsel bugs, Assassin bugs

NICKNAME: Silver-spotted skipper caterpillar
SCIENTIFIC NAME: *Epargyreus clarus*
LIFE STAGE: Larva
HOMETOWN*: New York, NY
LENGTH: 40 MM
FAVORITE FOOD: American hog peanut, kudzu
THREATS TO SURVIVAL: Wasps, viruses

NICKNAME: Antlion
SCIENTIFIC NAME: *Myrmeleon immaculatus*
LIFE STAGE: Larva
HOMETOWN*: Providence, RI
LENGTH: 8 MM
FAVORITE FOOD: Ants
THREATS TO SURVIVAL: Parasitic wasps

NICKNAME: Azalea caterpillar
SCIENTIFIC NAME: *Datana major*
LIFE STAGE: Larva
HOMETOWN*: Jasper, AL
LENGTH: 50 MM
FAVORITE FOOD: Azalea bushes, blueberry bushes
THREATS TO SURVIVAL: Pesticides

NICKNAME: Eastern subterranean termite
SCIENTIFIC NAME: *Reticulitermes flavipes*
LIFE STAGE: Nymph
HOMETOWN*: Richmond, VA
LENGTH: 3 MM
FAVORITE FOOD: Wood
THREATS TO SURVIVAL: Ants, moles

CAN YOU FIND THESE GUYS IN YOUR NEIGHBORHOOD?

Glossary

ALLERGIC: (uh-LUR-jik) having an unpleasant physical reaction (such as itching or sneezing) to a material that is usually harmless

APOSEMATISM: (ap-oh-zuh-MA-tiz-uhm) alarming colors, patterns, or behaviors that act as a warning

ATROCIOUS: (uh-TROH-shuhss) shockingly bad

CANNIBALISM: (CAN-uh-bull-iz-uhm) the practice of eating an animal by an animal of the same type

CARRION: (KAR-ee-uhn) the dead flesh of an animal

COMPOUND: (KOM-pound) two or more materials bonded together

DECOMPOSITION: (DEE-kom-puh-ZI-shun) the process of breaking down dead material into simpler parts

DUNG: (DUHNG) the waste material of an animal; poop

ENDANGERED: (in-DAYN-jurd) at risk of dying out

EXOSKELETON: (EK-soh-SKEL-uh-tuhn) the tough outer covering of an insect that acts as its skin and skeleton

FECES: (FEE-sees) the waste material of an animal

FOOD CHAIN: (FOOD CHAYN) a sequence of plants and animals used to illustrate the order in which they are eaten by one another

DUNG

LARVA

HYPOTHESIS: (hye-POTH-uh-siss) a testable prediction about a scientific question

LARVA: (LAR-vuh) a young insect in the second stage of complete metamorphosis (egg – larva – pupa – adult)

LARVAE: (LAR-vee) more than one larva

METAMORPHOSIS: (MET-uh-MOR-fuh-siss) a series of changes certain animals go through during their life

MICROBE: (MYE-krobe) an organism so tiny you need a microscope to see it

MOLT: (MOLT) to shed an exoskeleton

NAUSEATING: (NAW-zee-ate-ing) causing a sick-to-the-stomach feeling

PREDATOR

NYMPH: (NIMF) a young insect in the second stage of incomplete metamorphosis (egg — nymph — adult)

PREDATOR: (PRED-uh-tur) an animal that eats other animals

PUPA: (PYOO-puh) an insect in the third stage of complete metamorphosis (egg — larva — pupa — adult)

REPULSIVE: (ri-PUHL-siv) causing disgust

SALIVA: (suh-LYE-vuh) spit

TRAITS: (TRATEs) characteristics that make one animal different from another

Author's Note:

TRUE CONFESSIONS

Okay, so I admit, I may have gotten a bit carried away when writing this book. The idea of "kid" bugs being rude was just so much fun to play with! The facts are all true, but just to clarify:

- These animals should be called insects, not bugs. Technically, the term "bug" only applies to one group of insects, the true bugs, which includes the giant mesquite bug and the water strider.

- For this book, I had to pick from thousands of insects that do gross stuff. To make the cut, a young bug had to:
    1. do something funny and rude;
    2. be an example of an important scientific concept; and,
    3. live in North America.

- Surprise, surprise, I made up the whole "Battle for the Grossest" contest. Who's to say which behavior is the crudest? Which would you pick? Cast your vote on my website www.HeatherLMontgomery.com.

Artist's Note

While I've tried to stay faithful to the real creatures, putting these guys into human settings necessarily means taking a few liber Real insect eyes aren't the most expressive, s giving them pupils and eyelids is an obvious cheat. I have also lent some of them a set of t or anthropomorphized their limbs for the sa of a pose. In real life, of course, you're unlike find a water strider grinning or a silver-spo skipper caterpillar wearing a football helme (Though if you do, please let me know at my website, www.howardmcwilliam.com)